MADAGASCAR™

The Essential Guide

D1630175

Melman's sore throat is the longest ever

Written by
Stephen Cole

A large mane
and a larger ego

The world's most
glamorous hippo

Can a zebra
change its stripes?

MADAGASCAR™

The Essential Guide

Contents

ZOO

To: Zoo Keeper
Central Park Zoo
New York City

Dear Sir

I have now had the opportunity to examine all your animals. They're quite a crowd! Although I could find nothing physically wrong with the penguins, there was something about them that was very suspicious.

Alex the lion is as magnificent as ever – that raw steak diet is really keeping him in peak condition for performing. Gloria remains a perfect example of female hippo-hood, although a little jojoba cream in her bath might stop her skin drying out in the sun. As for Melman the "sickly" giraffe – there's nothing wrong with him, but by all means keep testing. It seems to keep him quiet.

Then we come to Marty the zebra... He's healthy and well, but spends lots of time looking longingly at that mural of the wild in his enclosure. I'm sure this is just a passing phase.

Overall, I'm sure these animals will enjoy long and happy lives within the four walls of our lovely zoo.

Sincerely,

Walter P. Thackenbusch

Walter P. Thackenbusch
Chief Veterinary Surgeon

6

Never has a bad mane day

Confident, upright posture

Tail carried at regal angle

Alex

He's the king, the champ, the *mane* man – the uncontested star of Central Park Zoo! Alex the lion is adored by the public, pampered by the keepers, and hero-worshipped by the other animals – and he wouldn't have it any other way.

"Who's the cat?!"

Steak-out

To Alex, one of the best things in life is dining on grade-A steaks. But he doesn't realize that steaks come from other animals – as far as he's concerned, a steak is just "a highly refined... type of food... thing" – and is not to be found in the wild!

The king

Striking a majestic pose from the top of his artificial rock, a fan blowing his mane, Alex may not be king of the jungle but he's sure king of New York!

Attention-loving Alex is always ready for his close-up! He just loves the "paparazzi" – that's the public with cameras to me and you!

Over the wall

"You don't bite the hand that feeds you," is Alex's motto. But he's also a very loyal lion. When Marty escapes from the zoo, Alex doesn't hesitate to risk his much-loved life of privilege by going over the wall himself in hot pursuit.

Washed up in the wild, Alex is glad to find his giraffe pal Melman in a crate close by. Always a lion of action, Alex plans to free Melman by charging at him with a huge log! Luckily for the nervous giraffe, Gloria washes up on the beach just in time to distract the frantic feline.

Paws hide razor-sharp claws

Soft and silky blow-dried fur

Ferocious facts

• Male lions are much bigger than females – the average lion weighs 180 kg (400 lbs) – that's more than the weight of two adult humans. The average lioness reaches about 125 kg (275 lbs).

• A male lion's thick, shaggy mane protects his neck in a fight – although Alex prefers his mane to be groomed to perfection!

• A group of lions is called a pride. Each pride is made up of several related lion families, though the males usually strike out and go it alone.

• Lion cubs use play to practise the hunting and fighting skills they will need when they're grown. Except for lions like Alex, that is. He's never grown up at all!

Marty

Marty the zebra is an adventurer at heart – trouble is, he's got nowhere to explore beyond his enclosure! Every day's the same: stand over here, eat some grass, walk over there. But on the day of his tenth birthday, Marty decides it's time for a change!

A party of tunnel-digging penguins surprises Marty. When he hears they're trying to escape to the wild, the seeds of adventure are sown in his mind.

Time for a break

Marty can't help feeling there's more to being a zebra than his comfy life in the zoo. He wants to get back to his wild roots for the real zebra deal! Maybe the break he needs is a break for freedom!

Zebras have a single toe on each foot.

Stripes extend under belly

Marty makes a totally stripe-a-licious entrance to the island, riding the tropical surf on the backs of two dolphins. This is one wild and crazy zebra – who's just crazy about the wild!

Animals away!

When Marty escapes into the heart of the city, his friends go after him – but it's not long before they're all caught. The zoo thinks they all crave their freedom and sends them away to an African wildlife reserve!

Wild thoughts

The zebra enclosure looks out onto a mural of an African landscape. Marty loves to stare at it and make-believe that he is in the wild. Running on his hoofmill, he dreams of galloping through the jungle, swinging on vines, and leaping over chasms – having a *wild* adventure!

Zebras can curl their top lips to enhance their sense of smell.

"Check out the zebra, takin' care of biz!"

Equine extras

• Zebras' distinctive stripes may help them to recognize each other – as well as to confuse predators!

• Marty is a Burchell's zebra. You can tell by his wide stripes and stripy tail. Grevy's zebras have dense, narrow stripes with white tails and bellies.

• A zebra's diet is 90% grass. The rest is leaves and buds.

Feet that were born to run wild!

Gloria

Perfect nostrils for snorkelling

Glorious Gloria is many things. A wise hippo who can see both sides of an argument. A caring friend who's soft and feminine – but tough when she needs to be. Whichever part she plays, she remains one hugely hip hippopotamus!

Hippo heaven

If there's one thing that Gloria loves above all else – besides her best friends – it's to wallow in warm water. It soothes the soul and smooths the hide like nothing else!

Gloria is a hippo with her finger on the fashion pulse. Even in the wilds of Madagascar, she manages to rustle up a chic bikini with the help of a crab and a couple of starfish.

Lap of luxury

The zoo animals are treated like stars – Gloria enjoys regular massages, gifts of fruit, succulent meals served on a silver platter... It's no wonder that she has never stopped to think what the world could be like outside the zoo!

Hippo-preciation!

Gracefully reclining – a favourite pose

- Hippos are the third heaviest land animals in the world, averaging around 2,500 kg (5,500 lbs), so Gloria need never worry about her weight!

- Hippos can float as well as swim. They can also stay underwater for well over five minutes.

- Hippos come out of the water to graze at night.

"The wild! Are you nuts? That is crazy"

Hippopotamus nostrils are on top of the head, so they can breathe while submerged in water.

All for one

When Marty escapes, Gloria insists that the friends team up to track him down. Melman the giraffe would prefer to wait behind, but Gloria is having none of it and soon persuades him. Whether in the zoo or in the wild, for Gloria it's always one for all and all for one.

The colour of a giraffe's coat changes if he's not feeling well.

When the animals wash up on the shores of Madagascar, Melman finds himself stuck in his crate. Alex decides that those cute little giraffe horns are actually head handles and tries to pull him free... OUCH!

Melman

It would be fair to say that Melman worries a little about his health... he spends more time in the zoo vet's waiting room than he does in his own enclosure! The idea of going to the wild fills him with horror – where would he get his medication?

Long suffering

There's always something wrong with Melman, at least in his head! Nausea, bladder problems, aches and pains... One time he even gets worried when he finds brown patches on his skin – he's forgotten he was born with them!

A sore throat's a terrible thing when your neck's as long as Melman's!

"Well, now what do we do?"

Guiding star

Although he gets nervous at the thought of leaving the zoo when Marty escapes, Melman actually knows all the best ways of getting around New York – as well as all the diseases you might catch there! Without him, the animals would never find Marty in time.

Tufty tail for whisking away flies – they can spread disease, you know!

High-rise facts

- Giraffes are the tallest animals in the world.

- A galloping giraffe can reach speeds of over 48 km/h (30 mph).

- Although a giraffe has the longest neck of any animal, it contains just seven neck bones – the same as most other mammals, including you!

- A giraffe can stick its tongue out nearly 45 cm (18 inches) – say "Ahhh," Melman!

- The patterns on a giraffe's coat stay the same all its life, perhaps to help others recognize it.

Front legs longer than back legs, for reaching the highest leaves.

The zoo

The Central Park Zoo in New York City is home sweet home for the animals. Their enclosures are clean and spacious, and they are provided with everything they could possibly want. Well, in Marty's case, everything except for one little thing – the wild!

"It's another fabulous morning in the Big Apple!"

Special "Alex the Lion" collector cups have been a roaring success in the gift shop!

Good neighbours

While the animals have their own private enclosures, they often hang out together. Alex loves bounding about between his friends each morning, waking them up before the zoo gates open. But although the animals can cosy up when they choose, all visitors must keep a safe distance – not all of the zoo's creatures are as friendly as Alex!

Information boards tell visitors everything they need to know about the animals, except that lions like their manes blow-dried and penguins like to dig tunnels!

The animals have fresh water on tap at all times. Most of them settle for drinking it. Marty uses his to put on a show!

Zoo, sweet zoo

Here's why Alex is possibly the zoo's biggest fan...

• Each day is filled with food, fame, pampering, more pampering, more food, more fame... Did we mention the food, fame, and pampering?

• His face is on an entire collection of cups, hats, and t-shirts in the gift shop.

For Melman, the vets are what make the zoo. They know how to treat a sick giraffe!

Home-boy Alex loves his enclosure, and adores being the zoo's main attraction.

• He has an artificial rock in his enclosure on which he poses dramatically – that *really* rocks!

• He gets served fresh steak every dinner-time.

When Marty escapes, Alex calls Missing Animals – but the operator can't speak Lion.

Pampered pets

The zoo knows how to look after its main attractions. The animals work hard during the day, entertaining the crowds with their antics – but when the zoo closes they are pampered like Hollywood movie stars living in the lap of luxury!

Taking a bath in front of hundreds of people may seem strange to you, but for hippo hottie Gloria it's all in a day's work!

Melman is never happier than when he's convinced something is wrong with him, so the zoo workers test him regularly. They put his mind at rest – and sometimes into a large hospital scanning machine!

Marty likes to stay in shape. Because his enclosure isn't big enough to really run around in, he has a special hoofmill to keep himself trim. He's a lean, mean stripe-a-licious galloping machine!

Marty's hoofmill settings include "trot", "canter", and "run like a tiger's behind you".

"This is the life"

Mane event

Alex is the zoo's big draw, so it's important that he always looks regal and impeccably groomed. Each night his fur is rinsed and moisturized, and his mane is washed in body-enriching shampoo before being blow-dried by an army of staff. He's not just the king of the jungle – he's king of the coiffure!

Massive massage

At the end of a tiring day, Gloria likes nothing better than an all-over body massage – provided her masseur has warmed his hands first, preferably by bringing her an exotic display of fabulous fruit!

When you're black and white and striped all over, it's important to look real sharp. So for sleek black hooves, Marty gets a little shoe-shine from the ever-attentive staff.

Melman doesn't just thrill to doctors' pills – he's a giraffe who's also open to alternative therapies. He finds a little acupuncture goes a long way. And with a neck the size of his, those needles *need* to go a long way!

Skipper

Skipper may look like a cute, innocent penguin – but he's actually a well-honed, highly trained, flightless fighting machine! Skipper's on a mission to escape the zoo with his penguin troops and lead them to the promised land – fabled Antarctica!

Flipper-like wings

Thick coat of very short feathers

"Don't give me excuses, give me results!"

Tunnel vision

Using plastic spoons as shovels and popsicle sticks as tunnel supports, Skipper and his penguin patrol have been digging a way out of their enclosure. They hope to reach the main sewer line, get washed out to sea, and escape to the wild. Unfortunately, on this occasion they only make it as far as Marty's enclosure!

Peerless penguins

• Penguins are flightless birds that walk upright on land. They waddle because they put their weight on the soles of their feet.

• A penguin's wings are unlike any other bird's. The bones are solid, making them stronger, and are flattened into flippers. Penguins use them to swim through water, steering with their feet and tail – although Skipper also uses his for unarmed combat!

• In snow, they may sledge on their tummies!

• Only two types of penguin spend winter in Antarctica – the Emperor and the Adelie. But don't tell Skipper!

Distinctive black and white appearance

Oil-tipped feathers keep a penguin waterproof

Webbed feet for standing upright on land

Flip-chop

Woe betide anyone who finds themselves on the receiving end of Skipper's flipper in a fight! This tough cookie's no rookie when it comes to action, and has personally trained his penguin patrol into an elite squad of action heroes. When the day of escape comes at last, Skipper will be well-prepared!

On the fly

For Skipper, being flightless is truly *fright*less! He's a sturdy swimmer, a wicked waddler... and he can always take the effort out of travelling south by riding someone else's ship!

Living in New York his whole life, Skipper has never seen a penguin's natural habitat at the South Pole. Will he like what he sees when he first sets foot on his beloved Antarctica?

Penguin parade

The zoo visitors laugh to see the cute penguins' funny antics as they waddle around their enclosure. How could they guess that each penguin is a highly skilled commando trained in the art of flipper-to-flipper combat and deep-cover espionage?

Kowalski – ever alert to the call of duty

Skipper – the proud captain

Skipper's squad

The swift pattering of webbed feet... the cold wet slap of a fiendish flipper... a grim squawk of satisfaction, and another hapless victim falls foul of the penguin assault force! Fiercely loyal to their captain, these penguin privates will do everything in their power to pull off their mission, whether digging a tunnel or stealing a ship!

Private – tubby tummy conceals muscles of steel

Mind over flipper

Of course, these penguins aren't just physically perfect – they have minds as sharp as a swordfish! Who would have thought they could override a ship's navigation computer just by jumping about randomly on the controls? Yet one plucky penguin private does just that!

Rico – master of five martial arts, including fish wrestling

"Cute and cuddly, boys, cute and cuddly!"

It's a penguin's life in Skipper's secret army.

Flippers high!

Humans give each other high-fives for a job well done – penguins settle for slapping flippers! But they have to be careful not to slap too hard. Two of Skipper's privates once forgot their own strength and nearly broke each other's wing!

The monkeys

Meet Mason and Phil, the zoo's very own pair of partying primates! Thanks to a convenient trash can just within reach of their enclosure, they're never short of the finer things in life, like a half-eaten bagel or a cold cup of coffee!

How rude!

Phil and Mason are miffed when Alex, Melman, and Gloria sing this birthday song to Marty:

Happy birthday to you
You live in a zoo
You look like a monkey
And you smell like one too!

But when Phil sniffs his own armpit and passes out, Mason realizes there's some truth in those old songs!

Knuckles used for walking

Chimpanzees' arms are longer than their legs

Area known scientifically as the "stinky zone"

It's a special chimp bonus when someone sticks a newspaper in the local bin. Phil likes to read the sports pages, while Mason just likes looking at all the pictures!

Cheeky chimps

- Chimps are the closest living relatives to us humans. Biologically, we are 98% the same!

- A chimp can make more than 30 distinct calling sounds, some of which can be heard well over a mile away. Mason's typical call to Phil is, "Get out of bed!"

- Chimps sleep in tree nests, out of reach of predators on the ground. They like to build a new nest each night.

- Chimps are very intelligent. They can even use tools, such as a twig for scooping termites out of the ground, ready to eat for their supper. YUM!

"Wake up, you filthy monkey!"

Mad face masks great intelligence

Crate ahead

In the wake of Marty's wild walkabout in New York City, Phil and Mason are among the zoo animals shipped off to a Kenyan wildlife reserve. And when Skipper the penguin wants to know where they're heading, only the chimps can help him – because Phil is the only mammal who can read the address on their crates!

Birthday party

It's Marty's birthday, and he's reached the big one-zero. But he's feeling kind of gloomy about the whole deal – another year older, and what has he done? There has to be more to being a zebra than this! But the others are determined he should celebrate anyway…

Piece of cake

Gloria, Alex, and Melman spent the whole week working on Marty's cake, a wheatgerm and Kentucky Blue Grass special with animal-friendly frosting! They even managed to get hold of a candle in the shape of a number ten, to celebrate his age reaching double figures!

"Let's make a wish, Babycakes!"

Marty tries hard to have fun at his party. He doesn't want his friends to think he's ungrateful for all they've done. So he acts enthusiastic – even when Melman's present turns out to be a secondhand thermometer!

Melman gets the party spirit – but makes sure his party blower is sterile.

You don't want to know where Melman's thermometer has been!

Gloria loves a party. She's super-excited!

Alex has already given Marty an "Alex snow globe" from the gift shop – a priceless present!

Chimps' drinks party

Phil and Mason are not your average chimps – they're not bananas about bananas! Mason enjoys a Martini cocktail with an olive rescued from the trash, while Phil cracks open a can of beer to toast Marty's birthday. It's not surprising that this pair should be secret sophisticates – a dinner suit is often referred to as a "monkey suit"!

Shocked expression – the animal's birthday song implies that monkeys smell!

Big wish

When Marty blows out his birthday candle, he makes a wish. The others want to know what he's wished for – even though it's meant to be bad luck – and Marty reluctantly tells them: "I wished I could go to the wild!" The others think he's flipped… They don't suspect that this very night, their bad luck will begin!

Melman points out that the wild is unsanitary. Alex declares you can't get steak in the wild. And Gloria's left speechless. Deciding he'll go alone, Marty sneaks out of the zoo, determined to reach the wide open spaces of Connecticut!

Breakout!

Rampaging giraffe hampered by drums and tissue boxes stuck on feet.

Marty breaks out of the zoo to take a train out of New York, and the other animals head off in pursuit. But the people of New York City don't appreciate their good intentions. All they see is a bunch of zoo animals running riot through the city!

Panicking passengers prefer to catch an animal-free train.

The stripy line

Not many zebras take the train, so when Marty makes it to Grand Central Station he causes quite a stir, clip-clopping across the marble floor! Being a smart zebra, he can even make sense of the train departures board. He's missed the express, so he'll have to take the local!

"We gotta stop him from making the biggest mistake of his life!"

A fearless champion shall arise... wicked with a handbag.

Humans can't speak lion language, so anything Alex says comes out as a ferocious roar. Most people flee in panic, but this super senior citizen is fearless. She hits him upstairs and downstairs and calls him a "bad kitty"!

Lion and zebra brawling like delinquents.

Clock the giraffe!

Poor Melman is not the most graceful of giraffes. Having already stepped on a musician's drum and some boxes of tissues, he skids on the floor of the train station and crashes head first into the clock above the information kiosk. And for *your* information, a clock on the block is hard to shift – even when you've got a hefty hippo hauling on it!

Rogue hippo hurries to catch up with brawling accomplices.

As the public panics helplessly, the police are called in to deal with the dramatic situation.

Alex is furious with Marty for running out on them. But when he sees they have human company, he cools it. He tries to make out everything's OK, but only scares the humans more. Finally, they knock him out with a tranquillizer dart!

Stuck!

After their breakout, the New Yorkers soon find themselves packed into crates! Alex thinks they must be off to a new zoo, and Melman worries that the management won't foot his medical bills. But none of them suspects the truth...

For Alex, being stuck in a crate grates! He's a proud lion used to a big enclosure. In the cramped space of the crate he begins to panic, and it's not helped when his best friends start arguing.

Thanks to some careless packing, poor Melman winds up upside down.

Alex flips when he realizes that it's Marty's fault that the animals are being transferred.

Marty has to face the wrath of a vain lion who's been robbed of his adoring fans!

Despite her best efforts at peace-keeping, Gloria can't stop the others from fighting.

All aboard

The New Yorkers don't know it, but Marty's getting his wish – they're *all* being shipped back to their natural habitat to live in the wild! But while the animals squabble over who's responsible for the mess they're in, others on board are preparing to act...

Airholes in the crates allow the animals to breathe – but also help some of them escape!

Plucky penguins

Penguins are good at hatching eggs – and hatching plots too! Enlisting the chimps' help to read the label on their crate, Skipper discovers they are off to somewhere hot and sunny – not Antarctica! So Rico coughs up a paper clip and picks the lock on their crate. Soon, the penguins are ready for action!

"Let's get this tin can turned around!"

Birds on the bridge

Once they've broken out of their crate, Skipper's penguins face the most dangerous part of their mission – getting control of the ship's bridge and overpowering the crew! Highly trained in the art of covert entry, the black-and-white commandos are successful.

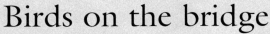

The ship is controlled from the bridge.

Flipper chop

The captain wasn't expecting any trouble on this trip – especially not from a bunch of birds. He was idly listening to music on his headphones when plucky Kowalski disabled him with a flipper chop to the neck!

The ship is close to the island of Madagascar when the penguins take over. And as they work the wheel in their own unique style, the boat bears south on a sharp change of course...

Washed up

When the penguins turn the ship around in search of a frozen paradise, the animals' crates wind up overboard! It's a scary ride, but finally they all make it to the shore of a strange new world – where an amazing adventure awaits!

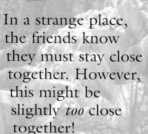

In a strange place, the friends know they must stay close together. However, this might be slightly *too* close together!

Mystery island

The animals have no idea where they are, although they do know they must be ready for anything. Could they really be in the San Diego Zoo as Melman suspects? In Alex's opinion it's more like the San De-*lame*-o Zoo! But then they hear... music! Where could it be coming from?

Even Melman with his incredible neck can't see over the tropical forest!

New arrivals

The animals decide to leave the beach and head into the jungle, still believing they're in the enclosure of a very large zoo. Gloria thinks they should find the people who run the place, get checked in, and straighten things out – but it's not going to be that easy!

This towering baobab tree is home to some very curious creatures.

Alex is very wary of the natural environment. He's a big city cat who prefers sidewalks to sand!

As these young trees grow taller and their leaves start to intermingle, they form a "canopy" above the forest floor.

Rainforests typically have a lush, dense ground cover of undergrowth and small trees.

"This place is crack-a-lackin'!"

Madagascar

Madagascar is the fourth largest island in the world. It lies 400 km (250 miles) off the east coast of Africa. The island is home to all sorts of exotic wildlife – including four rather nervous animals fresh from the zoo!

The animal life in the waters around Madagscar is very friendly, as Marty finds out when he meets four porpoises. But what about the animals inland?

Madagascar boasts 10,000 species of plants. Most of them are not found anywhere else.

Into the jungle

A beautiful stretch of unspoiled beach is one thing – a dense, scary jungle filled with weird creatures you've never seen before is another! Bravely, the New Yorkers put their best feet (and paws and hooves) forward in search of civilization. But what will they find in this tropical tangle of plantlife that has run wild?

"This place kind of grows on you!"

They're hard to spot, but over half the world's chameleon species live on Madagascar!

Alex's first experience of the jungle isn't a happy one. He stubs his toe, steps on a thorn, and stumbles through spider webs – and when Gloria sees a big spider on him, she beats him up while trying to get it!

AFRICA

AFRICA

MADAGASCAR

Madagascar facts

• The island was first visited by European sailors in the year 1500.

• There are 3,000 different species of butterfly that can't be found anywhere else in the world.

• Of the 238 species of birds known to live on the island, over half of them are unique to Madagascar.

• You'll also find colourful critters like the Madagascan leaf-nosed snake, sunset moth, day gecko, and collared iguana!

There are over a thousand different varieties of beautiful orchids on Madagascar.

Survival tactics

Zoo animals are never released into the wild – they can't fend for themselves. But when the New Yorkers find themselves stuck in the jungle, somehow they must learn to cope!

Melman

Being stuck with no vet care is Melman's worst nightmare – especially when he's convinced that everything in the jungle is poisonous! If Melman is to get through this experience, he must learn to stand on his own four feet. Luckily he has good friends to help him balance!

Marty

Marty is a highly adaptive equine, and he's hankered after adventure all his life. So it's no surprise he's quickest to get to grips with his new environment. He learns new skills, finds food and shelter, and looks after his friends!

Alex

Alex is too used to the warm applause of his adoring fans to know he's actually very scary! Having big teeth, slit 'n' slash claws, and a loud, terrifying roar will help keep nasty predators at bay – his friends may know he's just an overgrown pussycat, but no one else does!

Gloria

Gloria wallows in water, not self-pity, and soon buckles down to jungle life. She's good at keeping a cool head and smoothing over quarrels – she knows the only way for the group to get through is by sticking together. But she'd better watch her fear of spiders – she might accidentally injure her friends while trying to deal with one!

The lemurs

Life for the lemurs would be perfect if not for Madagascar's largest carnivores, the fossae. These irritating cat-creatures annoy the lemurs by barging in on their parties... and eating the guests!

In the depths of the rainforest, beneath the spreading baobab tree, the lemurs of Madagascar PAR-TEEE! "Ruled" by the loopy King Julien and his fusspot chief advisor Maurice, the lemurs' motto is, "Live for the day, for tomorrow we may die!"

Cunning plans

The lemurs have never seen anything like the zoo animals before. But could these newcomers be savage killers? Julien comes up with a cunning test to find out – he throws little Mort, the dwarf lemur, right in front of them! When the New Yorkers prove friendly, Julien is delighted. He will keep them in the lap of luxury so long as they protect all lemurs from the fossae!

King Julien the 13th is a ring-tailed lemur with a legendary fondness for berries.

Maurice is an aye-aye. He possesses the closest thing to common sense on the island!

40

Berry interesting!

Whenever King Julien gets something right or has a really good idea, he earns a berry from Maurice – ideally, an extra-delicious purple one! He rules by the powers vested in him by the laws of the jungle, and the province of the wild, throughout the known universe in perpetuity. Yes, he is bonkers... almost as bonkers as these lemur facts!

• Tiny mouse lemurs, like Mort, weigh as little as 35 grams (1¼ ounces)!

The baobab tree has a huge, water-storing trunk, and edible, pulpy fruit hanging down from stalks.

Lemurs like Mort have fingers and toes rather than claws.

• Aye-ayes use their extra-long, double-jointed middle finger to extract grubs and insects from under tree bark.

• Ring-tailed lemurs love to sunbathe sitting upright with their hands on their knees. Their stripy tails are used for signalling.

Best buddies

A ll their lives, Alex and Marty have been the best of friends in their safe and predictable zoo-bound existence. But the wild is a whole different ball game. Can the animals' friendship survive?

Ears that hear the call of the wild

"This isn't the end. This could be a whole new beginning!"

Ears that hear the call of a steak

Marty will always stick his neck out for his buddies.

Treadmill?

Back in the zoo, Marty sometimes felt that life was like being on a treadmill – you could run all you liked, but you never got anywhere. But a comfy daily routine suits Alex down to the ground. His motto is, "If it ain't broke, don't fix it" – but Marty has shattered it to pieces!

Alex has no idea where his beloved steak comes from – and has no inkling that, in the wild, lions *eat* zebras! Once, in his sleep, he dreams of food and licks Marty hungrily... not realizing that the first glimmers of his wild nature are starting to show!

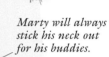

Revenge is wild

The animals know who's to blame for landing them in their wild, wild mess—the truth is there in *black and white*! When Alex gets mad and chases after Marty, the worried zebra hides in the one place he knows Alex won't dare go to get him – right behind Gloria!

Alex's powerful paws prefer cement to jungle

Practical hooves help make Marty's new home "wild, sweet wild!"

Two sides

Alex splits the island into two: one side for those who want to go home and the other for messed-up zebras who love the wild! But it's soon clear who's faring best...

• Marty builds himself a luxury cabin from sand and palms.

• Marty has a cosy campfire, while the others burn down their beacon!

• Marty gathers seaweed to eat, and makes kebabs for his friends!

• When all his attempts to get rescued fail, Alex says sorry to Marty for being mean. In spite of everything, they're friends for life!

An odd couple?

For all their differences, Gloria and Melman find they're really two of a kind when they are lost in the wild. While Alex and Marty are feuding and fighting, this helpful hippo and jittery giraffe form the glue that holds their friendship in place.

Gloria believes life is all about finding the right balance!

When the zoo animals realize they must find their next meal for themselves, Gloria takes Melman foraging for food. But the giraffe's cautious nature doesn't make the job easy – according to him, every possible plant she picks out is poison!

"We're together and we're going to make the best of it!"

Special bond

This pair watch out for each other. When Melman gets tangled up in vines, it's Gloria who helps him. And when Marty and Alex need rescuing, Melman offers to go alone – though naturally, Gloria won't hear of it!

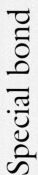

Rough reunion!

When Melman is washed ashore, he finds himself stuck in his crate. To his horror, insensitive Alex plans to ram the crate with a fallen palm tree! In the nick of time, Melman distracts him by saying Gloria's right behind him – just as her crate floats in for real!

Lost in the wild, Melman soon forgets about his imaginary ailments.

2-gether

Melman's and Gloria's experiences in the wild bring them closer together...

• While at first they side with Alex against Marty and his love of the wild, they both defect when they see all the fun he's having!

• They both agree that lemurs are unbelievably cute (at least from a distance, in Melman's case!).

• While Alex and Marty tumble about the jungle, Melman and Gloria prefer to relax together and get pampered by lemurs.

Bon voyage!

The animals have some wild adventures in the jungle, discovering more about each other – and about themselves – than they ever did back in the zoo…

Skipper to it!

With Antarctica falling short of penguin expectations (who wants to live in a freezing, blizzarding wilderness?), Skipper turns the ship around and heads for Madagascar. Will his elite penguin strike force be enough to save the friends and the lemurs from the snarling, savage and *very* hungry fossae?

It takes the lemurs to show Alex his true lion nature. The longer he stays in the wild, the more dangerous he will become to his friends – they're already starting to seem like fresh steak! Will he be able to control his wild urges?

Law of the jungle

In the end, Marty sees that the wild isn't quite the paradise he imagined it to be. It's not just about clean air and wide open spaces. It's about survival of the fittest and basic urges – like a lion's urge to eat his pals if they're not careful! Alex tries to cut himself off from the others for their own good. Even so, when Skipper's boat offers a way off the island, Marty won't even think of leaving Alex behind – and risks his life to go and get him.

The jungle may be harsh, but that doesn't mean it's time to rush straight back home to the safety of the zoo! There's a whole world out there to explore beyond New York – and even Alex comes to realize that it might be kind of interesting…

Marty, Alex, Gloria, and Melman learn something important in Madagascar. Nature may be running wild all around them, but it's in *their* nature to stay friends! Whatever new adventures lie before them, they will always stick together.

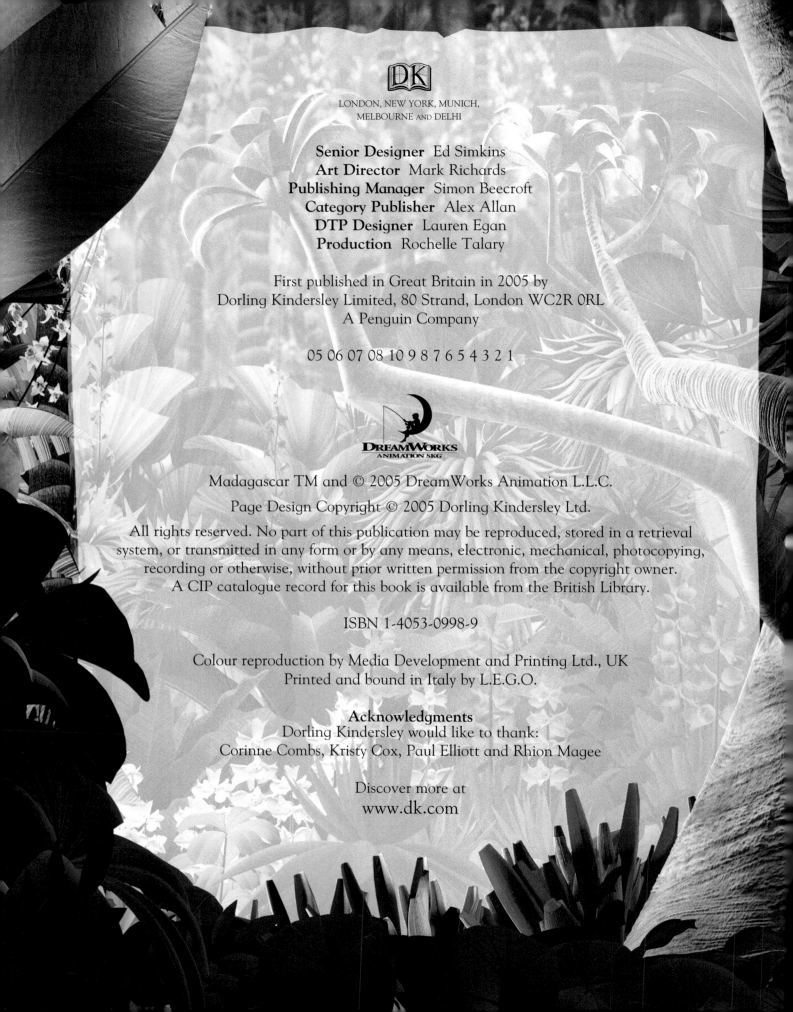

DK

LONDON, NEW YORK, MUNICH,
MELBOURNE AND DELHI

Senior Designer Ed Simkins
Art Director Mark Richards
Publishing Manager Simon Beecroft
Category Publisher Alex Allan
DTP Designer Lauren Egan
Production Rochelle Talary

First published in Great Britain in 2005 by
Dorling Kindersley Limited, 80 Strand, London WC2R 0RL
A Penguin Company

05 06 07 08 10 9 8 7 6 5 4 3 2 1

DREAMWORKS
ANIMATION SKG

ISBN 1-4053-0998-9

Colour reproduction by Media Development and Printing Ltd., UK
Printed and bound in Italy by L.E.G.O.

Acknowledgments
Dorling Kindersley would like to thank:
Corinne Combs, Kristy Cox, Paul Elliott and Rhion Magee

Discover more at
www.dk.com